Self-Care for the Chronic Caregiver

Jane Michaels

For my beautiful daughter-
You inspire me every day
Every moment with your
Strength and courage.

For my mother-
You encouraged me to
Love the woman God intended
Me to be and
Never let your Faith in her waiver.

Contents

Introduction

A little over a year ago, I woke up one autumn morning thinking it was like any other mid-weekday in western New York. Within less than a minute, however, I was sobbing uncontrollably, trying to catch my breath in between the heaving convulsions of crocodile-sized tears pouring from my eyes. Though it was late morning, and the sun was pouring through the open curtains in my room, the all-consuming darkness of my mind swallowed every inch of my being, and it was all I could do to cry out, "Help! I can't do this anymore, God! I don't want to feel like this anymore. Please take this pain away. I don't want to feel like this anymore!"

That was the first day of my absolute rock bottom and what I thought was the first day of my healing journey. Prayerfully, humbly, and gratefully I can look back on that day with tears of joy that He answered my cry for help and guided me out of that pit of despair. He has revealed to me countless lessons using the people that have been in my life, the places I've been, and the experiences I've had so that I can be of service to others, and in doing so, help others in their healing journey. And that brings me to this book.

Since I was a little girl, I have felt God's call to help heal others, in some capacity or another. It was only after my daughter's accident that I became a nurse, but I still felt a pull on my heart that I was meant to do something more, to share my story in some way that would help others heal. Nursing has allowed me to be a part of that precious moment in many people's lives, but on a drive home from the store one spring day about 10 months after my breakdown, I heard the internal call to start writing this book. As I began writing down memories and thoughts I had, and more memories began to surface, my spiritual journey blossomed into a whole new, and deeper, self-love that I never knew was possible. What began as a book I hoped would help others who also have been in a caregiver role turned into a book about learning how to love yourself. After all, loving yourself, your WHOLE self, is the best self-care you can possibly do, and then you can in turn, be the best caregiver for your loved ones.

One of the biggest lessons I've learned in my healing journey over the past year is to develop and listen to my intuition, or inner knowing (aka- that voice inside my head and in my heart!). So, the very evening I heard the call to write this book, I sat down at my computer once I arrived home and began to write. Over the course of the next few weeks, as I processed through stories and memories from my past to decide which to include here and which not, the meaning of this book and its title took on a whole new life of their own. You see, in the first few weeks, my focus was primarily to use my history as a billboard of what NOT to do if you are a chronic caregiver of a family member, friend, or have a career in the field of caregiving. The more I wrote, and the more suppressed memories that resurfaced, the more I realized this book is a testimony to my journey from self-abandonment and self-abuse to self-love and healing. The irony is that the title still absolutely fits perfectly, and I know you'll come to understand this as you walk through this journey with me.

It is my hope that as you read my story you begin to feel the inner knowing that you are not alone, just as I did. You matter, you are loved, and you are beautiful. Every inch of you, inside AND out is exquisite. And because of that absolute TRUTH- you are important and needed, and therefore, it is vital that you make yourself the priority in your own life. When you love yourself first, that energy is then reflected out, by default, to the world outside of you. This brings me to the mantra that I've lived by for the last year- Self-care is not selfish; it's selfless.

The healing journey for many people is a spiral in an upward direction. What does that mean? It means that just because a person may have processed through an experience or trauma doesn't mean that at some future point, it won't come back to cycle through in their lives again. However, the painful feelings the original experience evoked aren't as harsh the 2nd or 3rd time the same situation arises because of the healing that has taken place in the interim. The important thing to keep in mind is that there is still progress in an upward direction. I feel it necessary to mention this because you will soon find out there is a definitive theme when it comes to the men that I encountered in the first half of my life. Though I didn't learn about this aspect of healing until after the 3rd man had run his course through my life, I am still learning lessons from all my relationships, and I am grateful for each and every one of them.

Most importantly, my mission in writing this book is to help others in their healing journey, but in doing so, it is necessary for me to share my life history with you. Unfortunately, that history is littered with people who made choices that, to most, will be perceived as "bad", abusive, and in some cases harmful. Please understand that I do NOT, under any circumstances, wish to portray any person (relative or otherwise) that has come into my life as a villain, evil, "bad", etc. I know I can only ask you to try and keep an open mind and know that I have worked through my relationship with all individuals I do mention in this book. I have nothing but compassion for them in every story I share, and I ask that as you read through these pages, you try to see the messages I'm sharing with a non-judgmental view. Compassion does NOT mean that I have given them an excuse or permission for any traumatic experience they have inflicted on me. Compassion means that I understand why they made the decisions they did under the circumstances at the time, and I release MYSELF of any guilt and shame, or limiting belief that causes me further pain and suffering surrounding the experience. In short, compassion for them releases ME from further pain and suffering.

I know asking for compassion for others might be a point in your journey you have not yet reached, or maybe you don't believe others are deserving of, and I want you to know, I hold no judgement of you or your choices. All I ask is an agreement of mutual respect for others who are at different points in their life's journey and need to make choices, have belief systems, thoughts and feelings that (provided they do not cause overt harm to others) are in alignment with where they are in their own state of being. After all, we are all human, and love is the only way that will see us through to pure happiness.

One final disclaimer before you begin- to protect the privacy of my family and others involved in the stories I've included, I've changed all names, and locations mentioned are general areas only.

Chapter 1

Self-Care is Not Self-ish

The first time I ever heard someone tell me to take care of myself, in all honesty and seriousness, was in 2006 at the bedside of my then- 2-year-old daughter in the PICU at our local hospital. Katie had fallen twice in less than 4 days, leaving her with a spinal cord injury and paralyzed from the neck down. She was breathing through a tube coming out of her mouth and running to a machine that sat next to her bed. She was hooked up to IVs, pumps, monitors, cords, endless machines, all drowning my sweet little girl into oblivion it seemed. My rambunctious toddler was only able to move her head from side to side at will, nothing more. I apologize for the absolute morbidity of this scene I give you, but I felt it necessary to describe the circumstances my 24-year old, single mother self was in when the PICU nurse came on shift one evening and said something to me that has not only stuck with me for the last 18 years, but has been the inspiration for this book, my personal healing, and prayerfully, inspiration for many others who might read these words.

"Mom, you need to take care of yourself. If you don't, you will be of no use to her. I know you want to stay here at her bedside and stay awake. But if you are exhausted, when she does absolutely need you, you won't be awake enough to help her." At that time, there was a Ronald McDonald House facility in-house a few floors above the PICU, and the social worker managed to secure me a room there so I could be close enough to my daughter to get some rest but still be at her bedside should her medical status change at any point in time. This nurse strongly encouraged me to go make use of this facility and reminded me that I would literally be less than a minute away from Katie if I was needed.

I wish I had heeded her advice. I was so adamant about

staying at the bedside and not, for one second, leaving Katie's bedside for fear that it would somehow make me a "bad", neglectful mother. So, I pushed on. It's been so long now, that I couldn't tell you just how much longer my body allowed me to keep vigil at the bedside, but eventually, the body will not, CANNOT remain awake, no matter how strong the will is. Eventually, I did retreat to the Ronald McDonald facility for some rest, and of course, Katie was fine while I slept, but that nurse taught me one of the most valuable lessons I've learned to-date. Though here's one of the most bittersweet ironies of that lesson- I shelved her wisdom for the following 21 years. It's not only that I didn't heed her advice that day. No; I completely ignored and DENIED the truth of her words, and I inadvertently taught Katie exactly what I set my mind to do in the first place at her bedside 18 years ago. I denied myself time, pursuit of my own interests and dreams, self-love, mental/spiritual/emotional support, self-care- all in the name of pouring all that energy into Katie. The result was she witnessed a mother who loved her unconditionally and would move mountains to see her thrive, but who ultimately threw herself into a pit of despair so deep, she actually thought she was being swallowed whole by the darkness of her mind and soul. Katie has blossomed into a beautiful, successful, brilliant young woman, but she also felt the need to turn to her mother 18 years later and say, "It's your turn, Mom. You've sacrificed your life for mine, and that's no way to live. So now it's your turn."

Prior to my daughter speaking such words of wisdom to me, I thought the cliché, "beauty is only skin-deep," was the equivalent to what self-care did for the body. It is only now, over the last year, that I have come to understand how vital self-care is for every single aspect of who I am, both tangible and intangible. My journey has proven to me that consistent self-care can not only heal decades of self-neglect, trauma, self-abandonment, and worst of all- self-loathing, but it expands your entire being to heights and depths that reflect out into the world and heal others along the way. It has been the most beautiful, spiritual, jaw-dropping, mind-spinning experience to-date in my life, and it all started because I said, "Yes," to myself for the first time. Ever. Self-care has turned what was a very traumatically scarred, cold, short-tempered and pessimistic soul into a bright, loving, hopeful, and energetic spirit that wants to spread happiness and joy to others.

Though I've learned that I want to be the best version of myself I can be FOR myself, I've come to realize the best version of yourself is ultimately what your loved one needs and deserves to have as their caregiver. That was the message the nurse was trying to communicate to me in the first place 19 years ago. If you've ever heard the phrase, "You can't pour from an empty cup," before, you'll understand self-care is essential for anyone who devotes their life to caring for others. Unfortunately for me, I hadn't heard that phrase until recently, nor did I heal the aforementioned guilt that inevitably followed with anything remotely related to self-care until this past year. However, I've often joked with friends and family that my life's story to this point should be the billboard for all chronic caregivers on what NOT to do to prevent losing your identity, self-loathing, and self-destructive behavior. Then again, as I said before, I would not change any experience or any person I've encountered because they all have contributed to the person I am today.

As you read through the following chapters, some of my stories you may relate to, and others, maybe not so much. My hope is that some of the messages resonate with you and help answer lingering questions you may have or give you the courage to nudge you on your journey forward.

So, yes, you can heal. Yes, you can take your power back. Yes, you can dream again. Yes, you can LIVE again. But it all starts with a choice. The choice that I thought, 19 years ago, I was making for the love of my daughter and out of pure selflessness. The choice I made to say, "No," to every physical, emotional, and spiritual want and need I had in exchange for anything and everything I thought Katie needed. I can look back at a lot of decisions I've made over the past 18 years and recollect rationalizing them as doing what was best for my child, especially my medically fragile and needy child. Other decisions I made were out of fear of how I would be perceived by other people (friends, family members, the community) or of being attacked should my decisions be judged as being selfish in any way. All this, truly, comes down to one immutable fact- whether I did it consciously or subconsciously, I denied myself one of the most basic rights and necessary protections we are all deserving of because I thought in doing so, I was being selfish, not selfless. In refusing to meet even my basic needs over the years and only now learning to focus on myself, I've had to undo a lifetime of accumulated damage due to self-neglect, and misinformation and incorrect modalities of thought for my daughter. If you get nothing else from my story, take this with you and really think about it-

Self-care is not self-ish, it's self-less.

Chapter 2
My Father

When I began writing this chapter, I thought the explanation of my reaction to the PICU nurse's cautionary advice was fairly concise and simple. As I started to write this chapter, however, it forced my subconscious to relinquish childhood memories that I had buried so deeply, they had all but vanished, or so my subconscious thought. Little did I know that as the traumas associated with these memories began to resurface one by one, my OG mission statement for this book also shifted. As I released and worked through my past, I stumbled upon some other truths about my father (and my two husbands, which I will cover in later chapters) that have allowed me to have an appreciation for him and what he went through, despite the trauma he inflicted on me, my siblings, and my mother. Please do not misunderstand what I'm trying to convey. I do not want to make my father out to be a villain, nor am I excusing any of the interactions, experiences, or behavior I will share with you. What I do wish is that I can connect the dots of how his life experiences affected his relationship with me, which in turn affected my personality, self-concept, self-image, self-confidence (basically, all the "self";s), and ultimately, my choices, thoughts, and beliefs as an adult. This is not a way of assigning "good" or "bad" to what he or I experienced either individually, or in our relationship together; it just is from my point of view. All this being said, I must give a disclaimer for this chapter: some things I will disclose may be triggering to some readers, so please use your discretion and discernment if you believe it might be upsetting to you.

To begin, you should know my father was the eldest of 2 boys born in 1933 (d. 2021) to a middle class, Catholic, "Leave It To Beaver"-looking family. To everyone who wasn't immediate family, my father, his parents, and his younger brother looked, acted, and spoke like your average All-American family. However, over the course of several decades' worth of sporadic stories my father would share about his childhood, I came to learn that my grandparents gave preferential treatment to my uncle, especially my grandmother. Competing for his parent's attention and love was only exacerbated in high school by being ostracized for having the highest GPA, no friends, and graduating with 12 college credits before his classmates had even registered. The proverbial "nail in the coffin" for my father was when his first love, who just happened to be his fiancée (and no, it was not my mother), broke their engagement. As a quick synopsis, in high school, he met a French girl via pen pal program. Their relationship blossomed and eventually, they fell in love and got engaged. She was set to move to America, where they would marry and live, but when the day came for her to sail here, she could not leave her home and family, so my father broke off the engagement and ended the relationship. He never recovered from that heartbreak, nor did he miss an opportunity to recount that story to anyone who had active hearing. I wish I was exaggerating this detail, but sadly, I am not. He would tell this story repeatedly, even if Mom was sitting right next to him, to anyone who was listening, and with each recount, his bitterness and sorrow became more and more intense. I felt awful for my mother whenever he started the story about his French fiancée, but now, in hindsight, my heart breaks for him, too.

My parents met a few years later when mutual friends set them up on a blind double date. Because of his previous heartbreak, I can only assume Dad was now approaching dating from a practical standpoint and leaving little to absolutely no room for any emotion. Many stories of their courtship told by both Mom and Dad were dry, formal, and almost transactional, even for the era. Regardless, they married, and in my interpretation of how Dad felt getting married, it was more like another checkmark on his bucket list than marrying the love of his life. Still, they were married for over 60 years and managed to have 11 children together!

Before I make my next statement, I must make this disclaimer- I am not a psychologist or psychiatrist, nor do I have any formal training in psychiatry. Additionally, my father passed away in 2021. That being said, I believe my father was a narcissist. As of the publication date of this book, Narcissistic Personality Disorder (NPD) is diagnosed by a professional mental health provider using a combination of s self-report questionnaire and interviews done with said provider. Since most narcissists are, and will, almost always be in denial of their behavior, diagnosis of this mental health disorder is difficult and rare. And because of the method by which this disorder is, the abuse can go on, usually indefinitely, and from generation to generation (as was the case in our family), undetected and easily dismissed as "typical" or even "acceptable" social behavior.

So, because Dad was never formally diagnosed, and I still think it's vital to include my experiences and our relationship in the name of self-care and self-love, please allow me to point out what I believe were the classic signs of narcissism that my father displayed. One of the first memories that comes to mind is that he used to frequently remind us that "feelings aren't provable. They aren't facts, and therefore, you cannot rely on them." His "reasoning" for telling us that was rooted in his analytical and mathematical mind. At the same time, while he told us to suppress our emotions because they were unreliable, he was allowed to freely express anger, resentment, bitterness, and disappointment with all his children if his expectations or standards weren't met, AND he justified his emotional reactions in the name of Godly parenting (but more on that in chapter 3).

The second most profound set of memories I have is specific to me, as none of my other siblings experienced this particular set of circumstances. Of my 10 older siblings, I have 2 sisters and 8 brothers. When my mother was pregnant with me, my 2 sisters were already grown and moved out of the house, and my parents had a slew of boys between my sisters and me. So, when I was born, I instantly became my mother's "favorite" because

I was a girl and the last baby she'd have. After taking years of narcissistic abuse from my father, raising 10 children, and effectively becoming isolated because of all of this, Mom turned to me for comfort, support, and friendship. This angered my father greatly. I cannot tell you how many times, over the course of my ENTIRE life (not just my childhood) where my father said I was the cause of their marriage problems. I was the reason my mother was not "obeying" her husband.

Towards the end of her life, Mom's cancer returned, and at the time, she decided not to resume chemo treatments. She wished to go on hospice care instead of trying chemotherapy, and because she appointed me as her health care proxy, I obliged. Following her wishes, as difficult as it was, was made nearly impossible with my father berating me several times daily, saying that I was keeping him from "doing his husbandly duty to ensure her entry into Heaven." He believed it was his duty, as her husband, to FORCE her to comply with EVERY Catholic teaching, policy, and procedure on death and dying as HE interpreted it. Anything he didn't have an answer to immediately, he wanted time to find an answer to and became frustrated and irate with me when I tried to explain there wouldn't be time for him to do so. Despite everything, I remained firm in advocating for my mother's wishes and can rest easy knowing her dying process was her own. However, up to the day my father passed, he believed I robbed him of one of his spiritual duties to his wife and put my own mother's soul at risk of either extended time in purgatory or non-entry into Heaven. In hindsight, I know my father believed he had my mother's soul in her best interest at the time, and I do not begrudge him, resent him, or hate him at all for this. I understand now where he was coming from, and I have compassion for him that he could not see that his fear for the fate of my mother's soul was just a result of unhealed trauma from his own childhood.

I've given only 2 specific examples of personal experiences to introduce you to what life was like with my father, but it's difficult to convey the constant undercurrent of mental, emotional, spiritual, and sometimes physical control he kept us all under for the entirety of our relationship with him. And another disclaimer here: it is likely most of the hurtful and harmful behavior we experienced was my father's way of subconsciously seeking the love he didn't properly receive from his parents and family as he grew up, and then again being rejected by his first love. The self-neglect he showed himself and felt was, therefore, deflected back onto his wife and children. This is, by its very definition and nature, generational abuse.

You may have started to see how I was "groomed" to put others' needs ahead of my own, and therefore, may already begin to understand why I was so stubborn in following the advice of Katie's nurse that evening. Growing up under the rule of my father, I learned very quickly that if I placed my own needs ahead of others' needs, it automatically meant that I was being selfish, or that I was explicitly disobeying God's direct commandments to me. You see, compounding this guilt-laden rearing technique was our family's active Catholic religious practices and education for all 11 children. Please don't misconstrue my meaning by this statement- I have a deep respect for many of the foundational teachings I learned growing up in the Catholic faith. However, when a child has a narcissistic parent or parents, your sense of reality and how society actually works becomes very distorted. In any narcissistic abusive relationship, the narcissist gains control by first isolating the person(s) and then mentally manipulating them into believing that whatever reality the narcissist has domain over is the one and only true reality that exists.

By now you are probably asking yourself, "What has this got anything to do with the Catholic religion?" Let me tie these two ideas together by giving you an example- in my Catholic education (and it is also common among other Christian denominations), I was taught several times over, "Honor thy mother and father." This was a finite command. The only exceptions to this "rule" were if either of my parents ordered me to commit murder, robbery, or otherwise engage in some other behavior that would be considered a felony for either of them or myself. Other than that, I was to do anything either of them asked of me and never question any order, request, or demand. So, throughout adolescence, my father explicitly told me under no circumstances was I to EVER get divorced, even if my husband cheated on me, or told me he didn't love me anymore, or even if he decided to one day walk out on me. Divorce simply wasn't an option, according to my father and the Catholic church policies he quoted to support this dictate.

Hearing this for years solidified what I believed to be finite Divine truth into my mind and came with me into my first marriage. So, imagine my surprise, and feeling of absolute earth shattering, foundation crumbling shock when my father was trying to have a practical, rational conversation with me about divorcing my husband less than a week after I found him cheating on me (more about that in chapter 6). The point I want to get across here, though, is that a person who has been suffering under the abuse of a narcissist for an extended period of time will have a distorted view of reality. If their parent(s) were narcissists, they tend to gravitate towards partners in adulthood who treat them similarly to how they were treated in childhood because it's familiar. In my case, my father lost control of me temporarily to my first husband. Then, when my husband cheated on me, my father seized the opportunity to regain control by completely changing his position on divorce and gave new "evidence" of why it was deemed acceptable in the Catholic church. In doing this, he had now regained his place on the proverbial pedestal in my life, and I was to "honor my father" before my own needs and wishes, thus reigniting my cycle of self-neglect and self-abandonment all over again.

I've come to realize that as my relationship with my father developed, I subconsciously learned to avoid my father's anger, belittlements, and dismissals of my feelings in exchange for doing everything and anything he asked of me, hoping I would win his approval and love. At the same time, I mimicked my mother in that I believed my sole purpose in life from as young as I can remember, was to be a wife and mother. As I recall, I didn't have a personal dream of a career until I was in high school. So, after

18 years of these learned behaviors, I was primed to believe that by giving of myself to others, I would find complete personal emotional, spiritual, and psychological fulfillment. Now when I fell off the proverbial apple tree branch post-high school, I landed directly next to the trunk- there was no rolling away from the base, and I couldn't get any closer to the roots if I tried. In fact, for the next 25 years, I just sprouted and grew in the same tainted soil as my childhood until one autumn day when I realized I needed to uproot myself from the shadow of my past, remove the gangrenous twigs, and find fertile ground where I knew my soul would be nourished so I could grow and thrive.

Do you remember a few pages ago when I mentioned that, to a narcissistic parent, it is important to create and maintain the illusion to those who are not immediate members of the family, that the family is, in fact, the stereotypical "Leave It To Beaver" family? Well, one of the ways my father attained this public impression was to set nearly unattainable and high standards for all his children. All of us, of course, had household chores to do, and once old enough, after-school jobs. My eldest siblings had paper routes both before and after school in addition to schoolwork. Summers were almost always spent at the family cabin and property where we worked for 2 weeks to a month clearing trees or walking trails and general upkeep of the acreage my parents owned. I do want to acknowledge that my father taught me some valuable skills and lessons during these summers. In fact, I can't tell you how many times it completely surprises people (especially men!) that I am completely confident using power tools and yard equipment, and I can "McGyver" my way out of most anything. Since we spent a lot of time outdoors during these summers, I'm also adept at starting campfires, pitching a tent, driving a tractor and pickup truck, and it's all thanks to my father.

The high standards he had for us covered many aspects of our lives. For example, we were all expected to be on the honor roll every quarter, regardless of cognitive ability, personal stress, or teacher-student dynamic. In some ways, my eldest siblings had the most difficult time with this issue because my father was their high school math teacher. Not only was there no excuse for a sub-par math grade, but my father had a literal working relationship with every other teacher my siblings had during their high school years. The youngest of us kids at least got some reprieve when Dad changed careers and got out of teaching.

Even though Dad's career direction may have changed, his standards for our scholastic achievement never did. For example, we would have to lay our report cards out at the end of each quarter and get him to sign them before returning the cards to the school within a few days. One afternoon when my sister and her family were over to our house visiting, my father looked at my report card and saw that I had a B+ in Math (I was in 10th or 11th grade at the time, and in the Advanced Math class), and A's in all other subjects. To this, he said, "So, you couldn't manage to get straight A's this quarter? And in the one class you should have gotten an 'A', you got a 'B+'?" Even though it was in front of family and not strangers, I was still absolutely mortified. I was always very smart and barely had to study with any of my classes. I don't recall what the issue was that quarter that led to the grade of a B +, but I was still proud of myself until my father's remark. I knew I had worked diligently, completed all my assignments on time, asked for explanations from my teacher for the concepts I wasn't understanding, and I was even on the school's Math Team, too! My mother, God rest her soul, immediately called him out for being so hurtful in what he said about my grade. Ever the defensive narcissist, he responded, "I was only joking."

As a parent myself, I understand, completely, my father's drive to raise his children to become productive and contributing members of society. Where I know that he and I split philosophical ways is that I also want Katie to be happy, but because he believed happiness to be another emotion, it was irrelevant in his wishes for his own children. Therefore, every choice he made for his us was governed by his vision of what the "ultimate" version of each one of us would be as adults. That is, in part, why we each had private school education, were heavily restricted to who we could be friends with and pressed each one of us into activities that he found interesting and enjoyable, whether or not we enjoyed them, too. By that, I mean any activity any of us did was only at the approval of my father. For example, all my brothers were put in Boy Scouts and my sisters into Girl Scouts. My father was a philatelist, so he involved every one of us in his stamp collections to one degree or another. In fact, I spent countless hours (and I wouldn't be shocked if it was HUNDREDS of hours) driving in the car going from post office to post office collecting post marks. Additionally, he played the guitar, and he tried teaching all 11 of us how to play, too. Personally, when I was unable to learn the guitar (I think it's because I was born with unusually small hands), and instead showed an aptitude for the piano, and then for singing and the clarinet in high school, my father told me over and over again I would never amount to anything as a singer or playing either of those instruments and should just try the guitar again. All this to say, every activity we participated in outside of school served to give my father a perceived sense of control of turning us into his future high-standard adult children. His approach to parenting was practical, rational, and long-term and never emotional, spiritual, or present moment.

Basically, it was "his way, or the highway," as I'm sure many of you have heard a time or two in your lifetimes before. The problem with this cliché is that it causes inadvertent self-neglect on the receiving end of this statement. What I mean by this is that in hearing this statement, my subconscious internalized it to mean that whatever he said or ordered me to do was the correct thing, and therefore, logically, if my thoughts were opposing, were incorrect. To illustrate this, I'll expand a little using stories revolving around my father's insistence on us learning the guitar exclusively. As I mentioned before, because I couldn't manage handling the size of the instrument, and instead, I had an aptitude for singing and playing the clarinet, I joined choir and Symphonic Band in high school. For all 4 years, I took private lessons for both disciplines, earned numerous awards, participated in dozens of recitals, shows, and concerts, and even participated in my church choir for 3 out of the 4 years I was in high school. The entire time, my father berated me, telling me I did not have a good singing voice at all, and that I was wasting my time, as I would never amount to anything in the music industry. He even joined the church choir, too, and at the time, I felt he was trying to "outshine" me publicly.

When I was accepted into a SUNY school for vocal performance as my major, you wouldn't be surprised to hear that his remark was something like, "They must have made a mistake. You won't make it in the music industry, anyway." And I'm sure you can already imagine that out of all performances I had between high school and college, I can count the total my father attended on less than one hand; and of those performances he did attend, I received nothing but criticism. So, now it's easy to see how the receiver of constant criticism can, over time, subconsciously start to believe that, despite proof and evidence to the contrary, the narcissist's statements are the gospel truth. Over the course of my 2 years at that SUNY college, and a year spent at a NC university in their music therapy program, the self-doubt of my singing talent and musical capabilities turned into self-neglect, which eventually turned into self-loathing for even considering such a profession

To this day, I struggle to sing louder than a quiet hum in public because I can still hear my father's voice telling me I'm no good. I'm working on it, though. I continue to remind myself of everything I accomplished despite his words, and why he treated me the way he did. I remind myself that I loved my voice back then, and I still do love it. God gifted me with a tool that gave me some amazing experiences and memories that I will never forget. So, why would I want to hide that gift away? Why would I deny or worse yet, loathe something that has brought me happiness and joy before despite what someone else has said or done? What my father said to me all those years ago was a projection of his own unhealed pain and trauma. It was a reflection of his unconscious, desperate attempt to seek validation and love from someone close to him. And now, 4 years after his passing, it saddens me that he never knew he was loved. He could have ended the vicious cycle of generational abuse, self-abandonment, and self-neglect. He could have taught his children that feelings do matter and that loving yourself IS important, just as loving others is important. He could have felt the love that his children had for him, but that, ultimately, he rejected, because he didn't know how to love himself first.

Ever hear the phrase, "Do as I say, not as I do?" If you're still reading this, I'm sure you must have! This phrase came to mind when I addressed the financial shortcomings in my healing journey. From as early as I can remember and straight through until the day my father passed, the education and advice he gave me was the exact opposite of what he practiced in his own life. Specifically, I was given a weekly allowance for chores, which I was mandated to place, in its entirety, into a savings account at the local bank. I was not allowed to spend any of it. Not one cent. In fact, any funds that accumulated would be removed and placed back into my father's account if, and when, I purchased my first car. Simultaneously, he spent nearly all surplus funds on VHS tapes and VHS players to record HOURS of TV shows and movies, amongst many other hobbies he had. Again, this is NOT an exaggeration! In fact, when my parents moved from my childhood home into an apartment about 5 or 6 years after Katie's accident, my father had catalogued over 5,000 VHS tapes in his collection! His rationale for this hoarding behavior was that he needed something to do in his retirement years, and he wasn't spending the money on, "traveling, luxury or collector's items, or alcohol." The additional hobbies I mentioned included a growing philatelic stamp collection, computer equipment (such as software, hardware, paper, ink, printers, etc), books (also had over 5,000 catalogued when my parents moved to the apartment), model airplanes, and vinyl records. I'm sure most certified psychiatrists would diagnose him with a Hoarding Disorder, but my point is this- he was teaching me mixed messages. In forcing me to save my allowance and not learn how to budget or "indulge" in anything that brought joy into my life in the present moment, I learned to self-deny and self-abandon. Concurrently, I learned that he could spend, what I later found out was above and beyond their surplus budget, on excessiveness that solely brought him only temporary happiness (like any other addiction, hoarders get a dopamine rush when they acquire a new thing to add to their "collection", no matter what that "collection" is).

Now, fast forward 35 years, and it's only now that I realize the core reason I've had faced financial problems throughout my adult life is because I've felt unworthy and undeserving of financial freedom, and I never learned how to harness the function that money has in my life to serve my greater good. Instead, I subconsciously learned in my childhood that despite having a nagging feeling that something is off or the voice in my head that tells me, "You need to live paycheck to paycheck your entire life, and you'll never be wealthy," is wrong, I've believed that I don't deserve to spend money on anything for myself. But it goes way deeper than that. I've felt so desperate for other people's love since childhood, that once I became an adult and moved out of my parent's house, I started spending money on everyone BUT myself, trying to buy their love and approval. This was never overt behavior, and subconsciously, I justified it in the name of showing my affection for the other person. After all, if I love someone, and it felt better for me to give than to receive, than I should, right? Don't get me wrong. I still find absolute fulfillment in giving to others, but no longer at the cost of not loving myself first (more on that later!).

In addition, through no intentional fault of either of my parents (or society on a larger scale, for that matter), I incorrectly learned that the only way to grow my financial future is to keep my head down, work myself as hard as I could (and beyond the point that was healthy), and save every last penny I could, even if that meant sacrificing spending money on even the simplest, most inexpensive things or experiences that would bring me joy. All four of my grandparents lived through The Great Depression, and it is no wonder they passed this mindset on to their children.

However, the old cliché, "Hindsight is always 20/20," comes into play here when I tell you Mom and Dad taught us, just as they were taught by their own parents, life lessons based on what they were taught and the life experiences they lived through. How could my parents have taught us, much less encouraged us, to be entrepreneurs when their entire lives were about living paycheck to paycheck, scrimping and saving, and praying to God that the stock market didn't crash again, or rationing gas would be something that would only be a distant memory and never again a reality?

This has been only one of many frequent insights regarding my parents' financial situation that I've had, but it has allowed me to also gain clarity surrounding my own financial future. Yes, my father used money, in addition to a lot of other tactics and methods, as a form of control over me, but I have grown to have so much overflowing compassion for him. As I've said before, I believe he was desperate for love, affection, and validation, whether he consciously admitted to any of it or not, but the harder he sought it from his wife and children, the more it illuded him and drove a wedge between him and the ones he was seeking that love and approval from.

Not everything that I learned from my father caused me pain later in life. In fact, I have several life skills that I owe almost entirely to him. The first being, he taught me how to "make do with what I have," no matter what my need is at any given time. So, those who know me will frequently hear me say something along the lines of, "I can MacGyver that!" (For those of you unfamiliar with 'MacGyver', it was a TV series in the 1980's on which the lead would demonstrate elaborate problem-solving skills and techniques using the barest minimum resources). One of my fondest memories of this exact skill occurred shortly after Katie was born. I was knitting her a baby blanket using 2 separate skeins of yarn, and it was becoming a nuisance to constantly monitor and untwist the skeins to keep them from knotting together every time I switched between the 2 colors. So, I built a skein sorter (as I called the device) from a Lazy Susan, some PVC pipe, and a few pieces of inexpensive mounting hardware. My Dad was so impressed, he suggested I patent it! Even though I didn't follow through with that suggestion, I credited him with teaching me how to be resourceful enough to come up with the idea.

Another skill Dad taught me was how to use basic power tools and landscaping equipment. I have lived in western NY for much of my life, and winters here near the lake will cause you to have 2-3 FEET of snow needing removal from your driveway within a day! Snowstorms are a normal occurrence every winter, and therefore, you either need to shovel, use a snow blower, or hire someone to plow out your driveway. Thankfully, because Dad instructed me on the use of several landscaping tools, including a snow blower, I'm able to complete that task independently. I have significant medical conditions that restrict me from shoveling, and not being reliant on someone else's schedule to complete this task for me gives me a sense of pride and accomplishment. So, thanks, Dad! I'll take the win where I can get it!

As I look back at the overall landscape of my relationship with Dad, and I take a step back from that piece of advice given to me by Katie's nurse, it is crystal clear to see why I felt compelled to remain at her bedside and afraid that in leaving her, if just to get an hour or two of sleep, it would make me a neglectful mother. Discovering the rationale behind my stubbornness that evening was only part of the resolution. Stopping the cycle that is the root cause of that rationale in the first place has been something entirely different, but absolutely necessary in being the best version of myself and the best caregiver for Katie. As I hope I can explain in the following chapters, self-care, and ultimately self-love, is a choice. And the road to healing and becoming the best version of yourself starts with a choice to stop self-abandoning and instead, say, "I choose me."

Chapter 3

My Mother

My mother, to everyone that ever met her, was described as a warm, caring, loving, and kind-hearted woman. I've lost count of how many times people have used the word, "saint" when referring to her. She taught me so many things, including how to move mountains for my own child. She poured every ounce of energy she had day in and day out into her family, believing that was her Godly duty, and there was never any question in her mind to do anything else. In fact, she believed it was in the giving of herself FULLY to her family that she was to find complete happiness and fulfillment, and, quite frankly, I think she found her identity in the giving of herself to others. That, after all, was her life's purpose, wasn't it? Sadly, though, she never allowed herself the opportunity to take the healing journey to self-love before she passed in 2018.

Born in 1939 to lower middle-class parents with 2 other children, my mother grew up in "the projects", which were the poorer neighborhoods of her childhood hometown. My grandparents had another child after my mother, and because both parents had to work to make ends meet, all 4 children were often left with other family members after school or to their own devices until an adult relative arrived at the family home to help. Mom never divulged much about her relationship with either of her parents to me, except to say she was never close with her own mother at all. She was never taught many of the basic skills of becoming a wife or mother. For example, when she married my father, she knew only how to make tuna noodle casserole and scrambled eggs. Period. That was the extent of her cooking repertoire. She had no working concept of domesticated life such as how to multitask household chores, create shopping lists, manage a household budget, or even take care of a newborn. I believe this is probably because my grandmother had to work so much and had such odd shifts as a nurse. and Mom would never divulge why there was still a lingering rift in their relationship that caused such a neglect in her domestic education. My grandmother passed approximately 6 years before I was born, and so I had to rely on my mom's stories and fill in the gaps assuming what I believed would have been my grandmother's explanations of her experience of their relationship. Regardless, because of the "lack" of involvement in Mom's life on the part of my grandparents (whether intentional or not), I believe she internalized that lack of love and affection into suppressed and subconscious feelings of being unworthy and undeserving of self-love, let alone being loved and treated with respect by anyone else. This became my inheritance, the legacy

Mom passed to me unknowingly, and that I am working on ending the cycle of. I also hope that you, in reading this, understand that you can stop this cycle from recurring in your own life, too. The first step is always awareness and recognition of its existence.

As for the masculine influences in her life, my grandfather was, for the most part, a very fun-loving and kind-hearted man. Albeit I was young when he passed, so my memories of him are quite innocent and jaded. Again, stories of him from my mother are few and far between, but the one that stands out most is a conversation that occurred between the two of them when Mom was a senior in high school and had been dating Dad for several months. My grandfather allegedly said to my mother, "If (he) proposes to you, say, 'Yes.' Because no one will ever ask you to marry them again. He is your only chance at ever being a wife and mother. If you say, 'No,' you will end up an old maid." As good as my grandfather's intentions were to see my mother happily married and having a family of her own, he inadvertently communicated to her subconscious that she was in some way, shape or form sub-standard. Children, regardless of age, view their parents as authority figures and are dependent upon them for knowledge, wisdom, experience, and safety, whether it is consciously acknowledged or not. When my grandfather spoke those few sentences to my mother, his "warning" of future solitude turned into a life-long perception for my mother that she was not good enough for anyone- my father or anyone else, for that matter. What's more, the self-abuse that began that day inside my mother festered into a generational issue when the story was recanted to me. You see, my grandfather could not have possibly predicted that saying that to his own daughter might one day also have ramifications for his granddaughter(s).

As I listened to this story retold over the years, on more than one occasion, I imagined the pressure my mother felt to accept a marriage proposal regardless of her feelings for my father. Feeling that kind of pressure is one born in fear of being alone and of little to no self-confidence. I am not suggesting that my mother felt exactly that way and perhaps gave in to the pressure, but I am stating that is exactly what I felt and what I chose to give in to when I married. In short, it was like my grandfather was saying the same thing to me- I'd better marry the first man that proposes to me regardless of how I feel about him because if I don't, that will be my one and only chance at ever being married. I cannot say enough that I do not harbor any ill will or anger with any of my relatives, including my grandfather. I know he said what he did, thinking he was doing what was best for Mom at the time, and recounting that story to me also was done not to intentionally cause harm or hurt. The fallout that both Mom and I experienced from it was part of each of our own unique life's journeys. I am grateful that I've been able to recognize it for what it is, heal from the trauma my own path has led me through, and now share what I've learned with you in hopes it will help stop the same or a similar cycle in your life.

Unfortunately, the self-belittlement and neglect my mother experienced did not end with what my grandfather said to her. In fact, I was told the next story not only by my mother, but by my father as well- and several times over. My mother was an average student in most of her high school courses, except for math. She struggled a lot in this subject. While in her senior year, my father joined the teaching staff, also in the math department. My mother's math teacher, however, instead of tutoring her, or at the very least, encouraging her to get extra help, told her, "You'll never amount to anything more than a housewife. Best to stick with Home Economics classes." I am not exaggerating nor lying when I tell you that for the next 50 plus years, my mother insisted she was not capable of balancing a checkbook, completing simple calculations (which is a wonder, considering she ended up being such an amazing baker!), or even learning anything having to do with math. And don't even get me started with technology! The poor woman was convinced she was not capable of learning how to properly use a computer, iPad, cell phone, etc. until she had no choice but to be forced into it a few years before her passing. Even then, she still didn't fully believe in herself that she was able to use the technology at the most basic levels. I think in the later years of her life, she was so resolved to believe she was not worthy or deserving of anything that gave her lasting true joy and love, that it was easier to accept almost constant struggle, pain, anxiety, and fear. I am convinced this math teacher was just like my grandfather in terms of having no way of knowing just how much destruction his words carried, and did not do it intentionally (at least, I hope to think he did not, even though the 1950's would have made his comment typical for the time).

Her self-confidence and capability to learn new skills was one area in her life that I was humbly able to help her gain some ground in before she passed. After Katie's accident, she needed several months of rehab, but at that time, there were only a handful of facilities in the entire country that were equipped and capable of treating her specific type of injury and medical needs. This meant we needed to travel to Baltimore, and I needed a second person to come with me and learn how to take care of her complex medical needs. Mom was that second person for me. Over the course of the next 6 months, she learned skills that are typically reserved for registered nurses, respiratory therapists, and physicians only, and all of them had to be done on her precious 2-year-old granddaughter. When we arrived back in western NY and settled into our new day-to-day life where both Mom and I were Katie's primary round-the-clock caregivers, Mom turned to me one afternoon and said, "I never thought I would be able to do any of this medical stuff, let alone on my own granddaughter. I didn't think I was smart enough, but here I am, doing everything I was taught in the hospital. I am so proud of myself! Thank you." Even now, knowing that she finally realized what all her children knew all along brings tears to my eyes- that she was a capable, strong, and intelligent woman. Helping Mom gain this realization has allowed me to feel as though I've metaphorically broken or defied all the generational self-abandonment, abuse, and neglect inflicted by her teacher, father, and my own father. When they all said she "could not", "would not" or "should not", Mom DID and, in many ways, I ended the generational cycles for myself.

As I grew up and Mom grew older, one personality "flaw" that I became consciously aware I learned from her and am still working on is not being able to receive or take a compliment. What I mean by that is whenever Mom truly did something well, and anyone mentioned it to her, immediately, she would respond in denial or dismissal. For example, her homemade lasagna was the dish of legends, not just in our household, but in church circles, in-laws' dinner parties, baby and wedding showers, and every potluck or luncheon we went to. What made it so delicious was her made-from-scratch sauce that took 2 days to make. But no matter how many times she made it or how many people raved to her about how good it was, she would say it was nothing special. It wasn't just her lasagna that made people's mouths water, either. As I mentioned before, her baking was infamous; but again- it was, "nothing special." Her knee-jerk response was always to deflect the attention away because if she were to receive or allow any compliments, subconsciously that would conflict with the well-established lack of self-love that had already taken full residence in her mind.

If you want an ironic, yet complicated twist of events- I was told, from as early as I can remember, that I am the spitting image of my mother (as a child, this was in reference to my physical appearance). Oh, how I loathed being told that! The older I got, the more I grew to look like AND sound like her, and the more I heard the same old phrase or a derivative of it, "Hey, you could be a mini me of your mom!" Somewhere in my mid-twenties, I no longer hated hearing how much I looked like her, but I didn't necessarily like hearing it, either. It wasn't until after Katie was born that I really started to appreciate how much like her I was turning out to be, and the full force of gratitude hit me after my father died. I converted all the 35mm slides to digital format for family posterity, and in doing so, I came across every photo he ever took of Mom using the "old fashioned" style camera- from their courtship up to when she was approximately age 50 or so. The resemblance when comparing the two of us age-to-age was uncanny!

As I went through photo after photo of my mother, a bittersweet message became blatantly obvious that I find both comfort and strength in. I noticed Mom's vibrancy and excitement of becoming a wife at age 18 gradually fading and being replaced by overwhelming fatigue and hopelessness at age 40 due to having so many children underfoot and a controlling, seemingly unloving husband overhead. In many ways, I, too, lost my spirit when comparing the same age range, though the way it happened for me was vastly different than my mother's. However, though our physical features were so supernaturally alike, I had, in many ways, far exceeded all the dreams my mother could ever have for herself in her lifetime. Even though she repeatedly expressed her joy and life fulfillment in her children, grandchildren, and great-grandchildren, she always encouraged me to pursue my dreams and expressed her faith in my abilities to reach every goal I set for myself. I think, in some ways, she was able to live vicariously through me; to break the cycle of abuse and to rise above it all through me. I am so proud, and it will forever bring joy to my heart knowing she lived to see me graduate from nursing school. She never outright said it to me, but I sensed that she secretly dreamed of becoming a nurse herself. She did work as a medical secretary for an order of practicing nursing nuns, and I know she really enjoyed her time in that position, but I think she would have loved to pursue a career in the medical field, had she not had as many children as she did.

Most American children are asked in grade school to write about their favorite superhero. Now, after reading about my mom, I'm sure it'll take you only one guess as to who I wrote about, right? The thing is, when you merge my obsessive idolization of her with the adoration she received from everyone that surrounded her, an enormous void was created the day she passed that I was thrust into filling, willing to or not. Placing my mother in the realm of "sainthood" in everyone's perception meant that I had no room for error. At all. Not only did I need to embody everything she was to everyone that ever knew her, but I needed to surpass the expectations that I had subconsciously placed on myself to elevate her to an even higher place of divinity in the afterlife, if that even existed. Mind you, my father was still alive at this time, and still the ever-present influence on my psyche of self-abandonment, self-loathing, and self-defeating thoughts leading to feelings of fear of self-love or love from anyone at all. These expectations, though, were just illusions. Mom never placed them on me. Dad never placed them on me. None of my siblings or other family members ever said that I needed to embody Mom for them. The only person who ever placed these standards of how I SHOULD act, what I SHOULD look like, how I SHOULD sound, what I SHOULD say- is ME. I chose to self-abandon, yet again, in favor of stepping into the embodiment of my mother and the larger-than-life person I had made her out to be in my mind. It was a coping mechanism I could more easily swallow than learning to recognize myself as an individual separate from my mother and worthy of love for that sole fact alone. I CHOSE to take on my mother's persona and all the "perks" that came with it in fear that if I thoroughly devoted the time to myself, the person I found would be someone no one would love, or worse yet, I would not love. Thank God I finally did take that time to devote to myself because even though I do still adore hearing how much I remind others of my mother, I love the individual person I am separate from her.

A few months before Mom passed, she lived with us for 6 weeks so that the daily antibiotic infusions she needed could be administered by me instead of a visiting nurse. To thank me for that brief time she was with us, she gave me a plaque that hangs on the wall next to my bed, so that I see it every night before I fall asleep and every morning when I wake up. The message on the plaque reminds me that the connection between a mother and daughter transcends words, time, and distance. It concludes with the encouragement to love myself just as much as she loves me and to remember that she is always with me.

My individual identity is an ever-changing work in progress, but it is one that I am enjoying the journey of. In addition to being a practicing nurse, I purchased my home independently, and I'm traveling to as many places on my bucket list as I can check off! I also wear a charm with my mother's fingerprint engraved on it that was made when she passed, and I never take it off. I know that I carry her with me on the outside always, and most definitely, I embody several of her qualities, too. And as far as I'm concerned, if some of my qualities bring memories of joy, love, laughter, and peace to those that knew her, I am proud that I can channel her essence for them.

Chapter 4
Growing Up Catholic

As I've said several times before, I would like to make it clear the respect and appreciation I have for my Catholic education and upbringing. My relationship with God today has never been stronger, and had I not had the experiences I did growing up in that faith, I'm not sure I could even make this very statement. Having said that, it is my belief that some, if not a lot, of what I was taught in the Catholic church was misguided information. I know that will anger many people, but please understand, this is my perspective, and therefore, how I see it as it pertains to my story. What I mean by misguided is this- the core of all Christian denominations is absolutely inspired by and directed by God. I believe the Bible is the written documentation of God's direction. I also believe that God exists within all of us, and He made each one of us unique. This means that everyone has his and her own perspective, life path, principles, experiences, priorities, etc. Therefore, when you apply this specifically to the Catholic education and faith I grew up with, God's Divine words for me have been intermingled with thousands of years' worth of other peoples' perspectives, life paths, experiences, priorities, etc. At the root of everything I was taught in the Church and from all other religious influences throughout my life, including my parents, I absolutely believe my best interest and the fate of my soul was at heart. At the end of it, though, I've come to realize that best intentions aside, my personal relationship with God and faith has been made stronger when I've removed others' perspectives from my own and listened to the voice of what I believe is God Himself. And it was that voice that called me to write this book. It is being true to MY authenticity in accordance with what God has asked of me and has planned specifically for MY life that has made my relationship with Him and, ultimately, myself so much stronger and happier. The first steps in following that path, though, I believe were because I had foundations in the Catholic faith.

Now, I would bet my life's savings that nearly every adult in the world who has heard of the Bible has also heard the message that it is a book filled with messages of hope and love. In addition, anyone who has familiarity with the Catholic faith knows that attending weekly mass is mandatory, and it is there where you hear various Scripture verses read, listen to the priest's sermon that follows, and then sit, stand, kneel, and obediently recite the prayers. Most Catholics also participate in at least three to four of the seven sacraments of the Catholic faith when they reach the appropriate chronological or developmental stages. But speaking for myself, the only resonation any of this made in my mind or spiritual life was one of dying to self-identity and morphing into whomever and whatever the "All Powerful God" figure in my life at the time demanded of me. In my childhood, of course, my point of references were my parents, Catholic education in primary school, and the Catholic faith I was constantly surrounded by until my first semester in college. When I became an adult and moved out of the house and on my own, I began to question most standards and requirements I'd ever been taught, but did not realize in doing so I was still self-abandoning whenever I defaulted to the expectations of whomever I was closest to at the time. I did not begin to develop my own sense of trust or belief in myself, and therefor, self-love, until self-care even entered my radar that autumn morning when God answered my plea for help.

One of the fundamental lessons I remember about my religious education as a child was that God "knows all, hears all, sees all." You've heard a parent, guardian, or adult in your life say that very phrase to you, I'm sure, so it should come as no surprise that all I could picture in my head growing up was if Santa Claus somehow got promoted to Deity status. If God really knew EVERY thought and feeling, and saw EVERYTHING I did or didn't do, then there is NO escape. AT ALL. Which, to the little girl version of me meant that every single "bad" thought I had against anyone, or jealousy I felt because my friend had something I didn't have, or the little "white lie" I told to avoid punishment from my parents would go noticed by God and would definitely place me squarely in the realm of a naughty, evil, unloved and unworthy person. After all, doesn't God know exactly how many hairs are on your head? Does He not know the true nature of your spirit?

Some of you might be saying, "Yes, of course He knows! And the true nature of your spirit, of any child's spirit is pure and good!" But as you might have already guessed, I was firmly on the path of believing my spirit was sinful, evil, and selfish in nature. Unfortunately, this was another teaching in my education that fueled my self-abandonment issues. Believing that I was fundamentally "broken" because of my sinfulness naturally led me to the conclusion that God's Love, Grace, and forgiveness were things I could never have because they were only reserved for saints, martyrs, and angels- basically, worthy individuals. Again, I don't believe the Catholic Church ever intended for their message to become so convoluted, nor do damage to any of the children who had a Catholic education. However, sharing this experience is essential to understanding why I didn't follow the nurse's advice that evening and why self-care and self-love are so vital.

The Bible was never a book that I looked to for stories of love, peace, or hope. In fact, it was quite the opposite. What became very evident to me over this past year as I've worked through my childhood and early adulthood trauma is that in my desperate search for the "feeling" of being loved, somewhere along the line, I came to the false acceptance that my father was right, in terms of feelings not being something you can trust. My girlish, romanticized version of love that I had seen in Disney movies, in my dreams as a little girl, on TV and in movies, read about in books- all of it died sometime in my early 20's (and for the next 20 years or so). Since I associated my father's authority with the authority of the Church and central to my faith, I had been subconsciously shamed into believing I was unworthy of being loved or deserving of anything that would have been deemed "good" or a "blessing". Looking back, it's not surprising that I consciously self-deprecated (belittled myself to deny self-worth to myself and others) and self-abandoned. Instead of absorbing the messages of love, hope, acceptance, and faith that are so prevalent in the Bible, I heard nothing but shame, guilt, self-admonishment, wickedness, uncleanliness, and ungodliness. I constantly worried that I would take my dying breath without receiving Last Rites (the sacrament given before death to cleanse the soul of sin so (s)he would enter Heaven), and even if I did receive the sacrament, there was a part of me that believed I still wasn't worthy of entering Heaven just as I was anyway.

Any organization, regardless of religious, political, social, or otherwise, needs to have rules or mandates to keep order amongst its members. That's a fundamental principle I think we can all agree on. This is no different for the Catholic church. However, it touches on another reason why I self-abandoned in favor of someone or something else. To clarify, Catholic dogma is foundationally built on and disseminated through a laundry-list of rules. Rules are great for muscle memory in terms of patterns of thought, behavior, and even emotions. Basically, daily life becomes rote memory, and you start to numb out to everything and everyone because rules give you a false sense of security. What's worse is that your awareness this is going on is non-existent, as was the case with me. I neglected what my own soul was telling me, what God had placed on my heart from the day I was born, in favor of listening to what was being dictated to me through the rules of the Catholic faith. Again, I stress that I believe everyone involved in my Catholic education, including my parents, had my best interest at heart.

The rules of any organized religion, in my humble opinion, should exist to govern the overarching group that it administers to, not to dictate the daily lives and decisions of its individual members. This, I feel, is how I perceived the Catholic church in my life. Had my experiences been those of encouragement to listen to my intuition and learn discernment of the true messages of love, hope, and peace found in the Bible, perhaps I would not have made the same choices I did in life. Perhaps I would have advocated for my own needs, wants, and dreams without feeling guilt or shame in doing so. Perhaps I would have loved the person I was, at any given moment, instead of seeking someone else's approval of me or thinking there must be something wrong with me. Because if there really wasn't something wrong with me, I wouldn't be treated so poorly. I say these things as possibilities that could exist in a different reality, but for the woman writing this book, they do not exist, and that's okay. I'm grateful for having experienced the past I'm now describing to you because without it, I would not be the person I am today.

Discernment of the messages found in the Bible and teachings of Jesus's disciples was one of the most frustrating, yet crucial, skills that I was aware I needed to learn beginning in adolescence if I was to have any "real" connection with my faith. Growing up, I witnessed the differing ways my mother and father expressed their relationships with God, and it was as different as night and day. My father, because he was a mathematician and logic-based, would attend conferences and bible studies, read books on Catholicism, was a Eucharistic minister (handed out the wafers and wine at Mass) and lector (read the Scripture selection for that week in front of the congregation), and either played guitar or sang in the church choir. The only times I witnessed my father doing what I envisioned to be "praying" was at the dinner table every evening before we ate, every Sunday before Mass began, and of course the prayers during Mass.

My mother, though she did participate in dinnertime and Sunday Mass prayer rituals, did not have the opportunity to necessarily participate in the same activities that my father did, or perhaps it might be that she preferred to express her relationship with God differently. Regardless, I can remember going with her every Wednesday to a local church where we spent a full hour, just the 2 of us, alone in the adjoining chapel in silent prayer. The goal was, each week, to focus our minds and hearts on God and to cultivate hearts of gratitude. She also would participate in women's bible study groups and retreats with her best friend on a regular basis. If that didn't solidify how strong her relationship with God was, I knew that I would find her reading her Bible every single morning and hear worship music pouring from the car radio whenever we drove anywhere, even if it was to the corner grocery store.

When my confusion grew regarding the messages I was being fed from the Bible, my Catholic education, and the socialization I witnessed between my parents, so did my awareness that I needed to figure out a way to make judgement calls about not only what I'd already learned, but every lesson my future would teach me as well. As I've (hopefully) clarified to this point, I had a growing sense in my teen years that what I was being told from my parents, my religious education, and what I felt and thought was all conflicting information. I needed to sort out the right from wrong, the truth from lie, the left from right, as it was. It should come as no surprise, then, that it was my mother I went to for help with my questions on discernment. I wanted her to teach me what was the "voice of God" in my life and what was not. At that time, in my still-childish imagination, I half-expected her to tell me that I would hear a distinct, deep pitched voice in my head that would say something like, "Hi! This is God!" Her response, however, left me disappointed, frustrated, and confused. She replied, "If ever you have a problem that you ask God's help with and need to know if the response you get is His voice or the devil, you'll need to ask a priest, nun, or someone in the (Catholic) Church for help. They are trained to know what is God and what is the devil." Of all the responses she could give me, I never believed she'd redirect me back to the source of my religious self-abandonment.

Disappointment turned into anger at God when I became an adult, fueling my conscious AND subconscious belief that discerning God's voice was one skill I was incapable of learning and would forgo trying to learn in favor of "going it alone." Though I know Mom had the best intentions for me and wanted to answer my question, her answer left me wondering how she was able to discern God's voice in her own life but not be aware she was doing it. I watched her, without being consciously aware of it, develop an independent and intimate relationship with the Divine, one that brought her great fulfillment and happiness. This was my motivation for asking her to teach me discernment in the first place. To ask a priest or nun for help with knowing if God was answering my prayers, especially in a time of need, though it might have several religious benefits, would have been an exercise in reinforcing the problem that I was struggling with already- that I did not have the skills, knowledge or self-love in any given situation to know what is right and what isn't.

What I am realizing only now, as I recall this story, is that the problem was not my mother's response, nor was it that I refused to take her advice and seek help from the Catholic Church. In asking my mother for help in learning the skill of discernment, I was in a place of limbo. I was taking my first steps away from defaulting to someone else to tell me what is the truth versus a lie and towards relying upon my own intuition and guiding light. Without being consciously aware of placing myself on this new journey towards self-love and away from self-abandonment, feelings crept in that what used to be a beacon of light for my path ahead (my mother) were no longer there, and I would have to stumble forward in complete and utter darkness. That journey, as it turns out for me, was indeed full of obstacles, pain, darkness, and suffering. As the saying goes, however, "There cannot be Light without the darkness." This means that having been through everything I have been through, I discovered that I was my own Light.

In beginning my healing journey on that fateful autumn morning, I also started giving myself the time and space for reflection and self-care that I had been neglectful of over the past 21 plus years. The long-term effects had built up over those 2 decades, and my mental, physical, spiritual, and emotional health were all dearly paying for it. However, the most astonishing discovery I made was the immediate reversal of some of these accumulated damaging effects once I began self-care. Any changes that I made to my daily routine, behavior, or thoughts were always subtle and gradual, but always made a huge impact. For example, within the first month of starting self-care, I decided to take daily walks around my neighborhood. It was on these walks where I would clear my head of the previous day's stress in preparation for the current day and everything God had planned for me. For an overthinker such as myself, not having this "deep cleanse" of the mind done every day is like trying to pour water into an already overflowing cup.

This is just one example of many self-care activities that have revealed to me so much wisdom, insight, and self-love. I am grateful for every experience I've had in my life, including that which was painful and dark. I know it's cliché to say I wouldn't be the woman I am today without having experienced it (and that I've said it about a dozen times already in this book!), but it's the truth. Getting to the point where I can look at my reflection and genuinely love what I see has been an epic journey, and one that I am hopeful will help someone else find their inner Light to see the path forward.

Chapter 5

My 2 Husbands

At the risk of sounding like a broken record, I again want to reiterate that I do not wish to portray anyone mentioned within the pages of this chapter as evil, bad, or someone who should be retaliated against. Though much time has passed, and both they and I have grown into different people, it is in my humble opinion it is not entirely possible to make a comparison between the versions of who we are now and who we were then. To clarify, I cannot judge my actions, choices, or thoughts when I married either husband based on the person I am today. I've grown in wisdom and experience, and to expect my past self to act according to what I know now would be unfair. That ideology also holds true for both husbands, and all other people who were involved in the dissolutions of my marriages. Additionally, my marriages did not end because of the poor choices of only one person. I own the mistakes I made in both relationships, and it is never all one person's fault. So, to protect the identities of both exes, my first husband will be known as Seth, and my second husband as Ben.

I met Seth in an AOL chatroom while attending a 4-year school in my sophomore year. No longer an amateur at the independence college life instantly grants you, I was still knee-deep working 2 part-time jobs and taking a full course load that autumn semester when I wandered into a virtual cafe. It also begs to be mentioned that I had been berated the previous summer by my father in hearing him say, "If a woman eventually wants to marry and have children, then she should not be going to college. She belongs in the home. Husbands and children should not have wives and a mother that works or has a career." Anyway, my desperation in finding validation, attention, and even the slightest sign of something that resembled love was at an all-time high when Seth and I began chatting. Our virtual conversations quickly progressed to phone calls, but because he was in the army and stationed out-of-state at the time, I met his family (who lived locally) before I met him in person. Our relationship progressed quickly, and we were engaged within 6 months of our first online chat.

We were able to spend time with each other a few times before we married, whether it be that I flew out to be with him where he was stationed or he came home on leave. During our courtship, however, there were a few personality characteristics that I would dub "minor red flag" behaviors, or things he would say, that made the angel-on-my-shoulder tell me NOT to marry the man. But being so self-abandoning, self-hating, and desperate for a man to love me at the time, I ignored that angel and married him anyway. Those red flags, however, turned into red sirens, billboards, and bombs nearly overnight.

As a first-time bride, and a devotedly raised Catholic bride at that, I believed it was my duty to "submit (myself) to (my) husband". Having the example of my parents' marriage and literally no formal education on what a respectful, loving marriage looks like, I blindly accepted the physical, psychological, and emotional abuse that I was subjected to during our relationship. Additionally, Dad mentioned to me during my adolescence that "rape does not and cannot exist in a marriage." It wasn't until I separated from Ben that I realized the horrific inaccuracy and trauma that statement alone had caused me.

Ever since I was a child, my ultimate dream had been to be a wife and mother, but it never occurred to me what the cost would be to achieve that dream. Even though I witnessed my mother being subjected to my father's narcissistic mistreatment in their marriage, I still had the idealistic fairytale Prince Charming husband in my fantasy and never factored in a future that would mirror reality in any way. I CHOSE to turn my back on my own family, despite them having reservations and legitimate concerns about Seth. I CHOSE to ignore the warning signs and voice of my guardian angel. I CHOSE to believe that Seth was not abusive, cheating on me, or manipulating me in any way during our relationship. I CHOSE to continue to believe that he was my Prince Charming, even when the evidence was blatantly obvious and couldn't be explained away anymore. I clung onto my childhood fantasy until my world literally came crashing down around me. I CHOSE to self-abandon in favor of a man and marriage that didn't exist. You're probably wondering when that happened and why I continued to stay? First, let me give you a little more context before I tell you.

Remember the second part of my childhood dream- to become a mother? Well, once Seth was discharged from the military, I was eager to start our family. He, however, was not. Unbeknownst to me at the time, almost as soon as he returned home, he started having affairs. Because I was naïve to this fact, I pressured him into starting a family, and I think God knew exactly what He was doing with the medical condition I have that makes it difficult for me to conceive. Shortly after his discharge, I sustained a work-related injury requiring surgical repair, placing our family plans on hold. Once I had sufficiently healed from this surgery, however, I became pregnant with Katie almost immediately. It was when I came home early from college classes three months later that I came face-to-face with my world crashing down around me. I caught him having one of those affairs. What followed from that moment forward will remain private, and I am often asked why I ignored the warning signs that came well before this day even happened. At the opening of this chapter, I mentioned that I cannot, and will not, judge myself or anyone else in the past by a standard that I have today. Hindsight is always 20/20, but unfortunately, current sight often suffers from cataracts. I couldn't see the "bigger picture" of what was going on at the time I was in that situation, and for good reason. Had I left Seth before that day, I might not have Katie today.

An important aspect of healing from trauma is that it is an upward and continual journey, and I am grateful I no longer look back on memories of my marriage to Seth with anger, sorrow, or torment. I see the day I returned home from college classes as a pivot-point in my life. I see it as an opportunity I was given to stop self-abandoning. All the warning signs I had been ignoring up to that point were no longer avoidable, and God was shutting the door on that chapter of my life, only to open so many more windows. The thing is it took a while for the cataracts to clear from my eyes for me to see those open windows.

I moved back in with my parents immediately and began divorce proceedings, all while my pregnancy with Katie continued. I am grateful beyond words that Katie was born healthy, full-term, and with (no-joke!) a smile on her face despite having spent 9 months growing in a very stress-filled environment. Mom was my labor coach, and the second Katie was born, I turned to my mother and said, "I did it. I'm finally a mother." Though that may have seemed such an innocent statement at the time, it was such a profound act of self-love now that I look back on it. That childhood dream of becoming a mother is a calling that was placed on my heart, I believe, by God. To ignore it or deny myself that dream would be an act of self-hate. Fulfilling my motherhood dream, even though it was at the cost of abuse and trauma, was, in the end, an act of self-love. What's more, I've had several people ask me over the years if I would marry Seth again, given the chance, or would I repeat the same choices I made all those years ago? And the answer is a resounding, "Yes!" Had I not married Seth, I might never have become a mother, and I certainly would not have my beautiful Katie. She is worth every bit of struggle and difficulty I went through, and so much more, and I would do it all over again, tenfold.

From the day Katie was born, Seth did not want to be a part of her life, but I still felt it was important for her to have a father, as a man could teach her things that I could not. Though we continued to live with my parents until Katie was approximately 3 years old, I did not like that my own father served as her father-figure. I had made some progress in my own healing journey in terms of breaking the control my father had over me, but it was negligible. I was aware enough to know I did not want Katie to grow up feeling the same pressure, self-hate, and control that I did. I knew I had to find a man that was loving, kind, and genuine.

So, soon after we had settled into daily life routine after Katie's accident, and I had applied to nursing school, I decided to try dating again via an online service. Imagine my surprise when an old friend from my early college days, and before I met Seth, showed up as a match! Re-enter Ben back into my life! Ben and I met a few months prior to Seth and I meeting, had become instant friends, but lost our friendship just as quickly once Seth and I married. Now, years later and with the dating service matching us up, we picked up where we had left off, and the chemistry we had almost a decade prior was still there.

That friendship was something that we both cherished deeply, and though I wanted to explore a relationship with him, he was adamant that we do not. For several weeks, we talked about how we each felt; he did not want to risk losing our friendship if the relationship did not work out, and I was convinced that if we did not date, we would be throwing away the love of a lifetime. Additionally, he did repeatedly say that he liked to live the bachelor lifestyle. In retrospect, I pressured Ben into a relationship that he was not ready for.

We dated for a little over a year before getting engaged, and we also had the history prior to my first marriage together. Ben adored Katie, and I had made it clear to him I wanted to marry someone who was willing to fill that father roll in her life. Though I give Ben credit for being honest about his preferred lifestyle choices, there were several other "warning signs" that I ignored, just like I had with Seth. One difference that I thought justified my choices this time around was that we attended pre-marital counselling, and I believed Ben had been educated by both the cleric and me enough to know what a committed, loving, and mature marriage required. At the same time, I thought I had healed from my first marriage and my relationship with Dad. But alas, I was in a self-righteous, pious frame of reference, trying to control my life and everyone in it. I don't have to include many detailed stories for you to know that our marriage quickly turned our long-standing friendship into a bitter resentment of each other.

I admit I did not know Ben's exact meaning behind his statement that he preferred the "bachelor lifestyle," but it didn't take me long to understand. Once we reconnected as friends, I quickly learned it meant he liked to date a lot of women simultaneously, and even have "friends with benefits". During the weeks we discussed the possibility of having a relationship, I addressed this lifestyle choice of his and made it a requirement if we dated that all intimate relationships with other females would immediately cease. In establishing this boundary, I think this was the first time I showed myself an act of self-love and didn't self-abandon when it came to relationships. The thing with boundaries is that they are a two-part process- establishment and enforcement. I completed the first part in verbally setting the boundary, but it took me nearly 7 years to enforce it by standing up for myself instead of tolerating being cheated on.

Over the course of my marriage to Ben, there was tremendous amounts of psychological, emotional, and some physical abuse. Again, I do not wish to villainize him, and I completely own that I made many mistakes and caused hurt for him, too. Though I haven't had the same question asking if I would marry Ben again given the chance, like I did Seth, my answer still would be, "Yes." The psychological trauma I experienced was the most difficult part of my second marriage, and it has, without a doubt, taught me so much about self-love and self-care and its importance in my life. The list of discoveries I've made about life, myself, and others is significant, but perhaps the most important is how resilient and independent I am. It was because of my marriage to Ben that fallen in love with these aspects of myself, and I am grateful for that.

I mentioned that while in pre-marital counseling with Ben, I believed I had healed from my marriage to Seth and my relationship with Dad. I was using all the experience, life-lessons, and knowledge I had gained from those 2 relationships alone as a platform of feeling like I had all the answers for whatever this marriage threw at me. However, almost from the start, I began defaulting to my usual people-pleasing-tactics- defaulting to Ben making ALL the decisions regardless of the gravity of the situation; sacrificing my preferences, dreams, and desires for his; accepting blame for things that I never had any association with; and the list goes on and on. Let me be clear- these behaviors were MY choices. In hindsight, I recognize that these choices were based on thought processes and behaviors that have been subconsciously ingrained in me since childhood, and I'm working on unlearning them. Taking ownership of my own behavior, however, has also given me back personal power.

Even though I believed I was acting in love whenever I did any of the people-pleasing behaviors mentioned previously, it wasn't until recently I discovered these are self-hating behaviors and are the exact opposite of self-love. Throughout my entire adolescence and both marriages (especially to Seth), I could never understand why the men in my life treated me so poorly the more I loved them. It was like the better I treated them, the more of my heart I gave them, the worse they treated me and the more abuse I suffered. I can't tell you how many times the thought, "I just don't understand what's wrong with me," went through my head. I can't tell you how many years I spent between these three men thinking I was going crazy. I can't tell you how many nights I cried myself to sleep hoping I would wake up the next morning in a different reality where my father or husband would be the man in my daydreams. Yet every morning, I would awake to more of the same living nightmare. Or so I thought at the time. What it turned out to be, in the end, was more lessons in learning to love the person God intended me to be. More lessons in gaining inner strength, finding the courage to devote time and energy to the person I was made to be, and releasing the oppression of others who wanted to keep me from becoming that person.

I'm sure some of you are, as you are reading this, going through this exact same scenario or something similar. Or maybe you've felt this same way before. What I will tell you is what I was told many years ago by a dear counselor and has stayed with me for all this time- You are NOT crazy. You are LOVED. You are WANTED and NEEDED. You are the MOST IMPORTANT person in your life. Be HERE. Be PRESENT in THIS moment. Tomorrow is not promised. Yesterday is a memory. Your presence, HERE and NOW, is PRICELESS!

I hope you've come to understand at this point in the book one of the common threads running through all the chapters- self-care is not only the solution to finding self-love, but also the proactive way to build self-love. They go hand-in-hand. For those of you who are called to give of yourselves in the service of others as caregivers, like I am, it is especially important to make self-care a top priority. Your loved ones and those who depend on you deserve the best version you can possibly be. Self-care and self-love are how you attain that best version of yourself. Self-care is not self-ish, it's self-less!

Chapter 6

Conclusion

If I may, let's go back to Katie's hospital room, 21 years ago and try to imagine yourself in the room with the 24-year-old version of me and the evening nurse who has just given me this profound piece of advice. Literally, close your eyes, and envision yourself in the room with me. The nurse has just suggested I go get some rest so that I'm alert and well should Katie need me at a later point. Do the nurse's words resonate with you, too? Having read this book, and perhaps resonating with some of my thoughts or stories, does my reluctance to follow her advice and the guilt in doing so also resonate with you? Have you ever been through a similar situation or had feelings like that 24-year-old version of me? Most importantly, what is your response to the nurse's suggestion? Do you heed her advice? Or do you remain at the bedside holding vigil like I did because you falsely believe it makes you a super-parent?

Devoting time and energy to fulfilling even the most basic of my needs, even back then, would not have required much at all. My cataracts, however, were so thick and cloudy my chances of seeing that truth, even as it was being channeled through the nurse's advice, were virtually nonexistent. I will die on my hill that I would not change any events of my past, but that does not mean I still don't wonder now and again how much "better care" I could have given Katie had I gotten just a few hours' sleep. If nothing else, my enormous gratitude for the value of self-care the nurse taught me that evening has removed any last inkling of guilt that may still linger for not listening to her in the first place.

I mentioned before that self-care is the cure for self-hate, self-abandonment and self-devaluation. It is also the prevention for these personal rejections. The road to healing from trauma, abuse, neglect, and/or misinformation can be a long, painful, and very confusing journey. At times, it was overwhelming, and I didn't know if I could handle processing through the worst of my memories and trauma. Yet I noticed a surprising theme in this healing journey- no matter the ebb and flow of what I was going through, I always had a support system surrounding me in my family and friends, and none of whom chastised me for finally devoting the time and energy I was into myself. In fact, they applauded me for doing it and even asking me what my secret was that I seemed so happy all the time. In all seriousness, I had perfect strangers complimenting me on how cheerful I was and that I seemed to light up a room just walking into it!

The devotion to Katie and every one of her needs since her accident 19 years ago has been, like she said, my life's purpose. However, as I compare what life was like then to the day I began self-care, the differences are like night and day. Before self-care was a priority for me, I was just surviving. Yes, I was advocating for Katie. I was fighting for services, equipment, basic medical coverage. But she was my focus from the second I awoke until the second my mind relaxed and I drifted to sleep at night, and there was never a thought for myself or my own needs in between. Not really. Again, I absolutely, unequivocally love Katie with every fiber of my being and would not change any choice I've ever made for her. Yet, there were plenty of spare minutes in the last 19 years that I could have devoted to myself. Ten more minutes of sleep, 5 extra minutes in the shower, or taking the scenic route home that added 3 minutes to my commute time- all these self-care acts are simple but monumentally effective in giving my mind and soul a rest. Accumulated over time, they have healed so much hurt and pain, and what's more- given me a bright, hopeful outlook on life and given Katie the best caregiving mother she can have, and quite frankly, DESERVES to have!

www.ingramcontent.com/pod-product-compliance
Lightning Source LLC
Chambersburg PA
CBHW050814160726
48004CB00002B/843

* 9 7 9 8 8 9 7 6 6 5 1 7 4 *